Scott and the Gladiator

Scott looked in the old mirror.

Someone looked back at him.

The boy in the mirror looked a bit
like Scott but he wasn't Scott and
he was wearing very strange clothes.

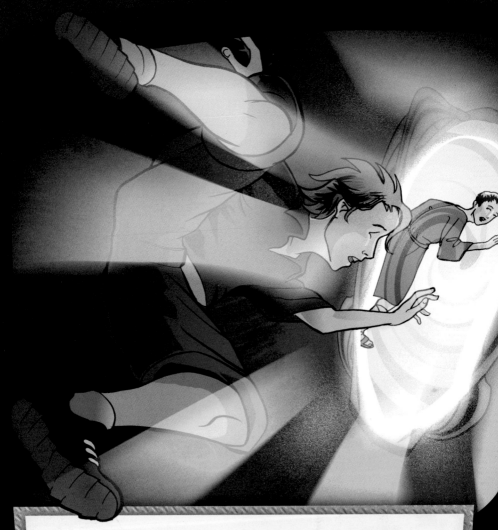

"Come on," said the boy in the mirror,
"or we'll be late."
Scott stepped forward and felt himself
falling into the mirror!

Scott looked around. He was in a huge arena. There were lots and lots of people. They were cheering and shouting.

Then a man came up to them.

"Marcus," he said, "you are late. Is this the new gladiator?"

"Yes, Master," said Marcus.

"Is he brave and strong?" said the man.

"Very brave and strong," said Marcus.

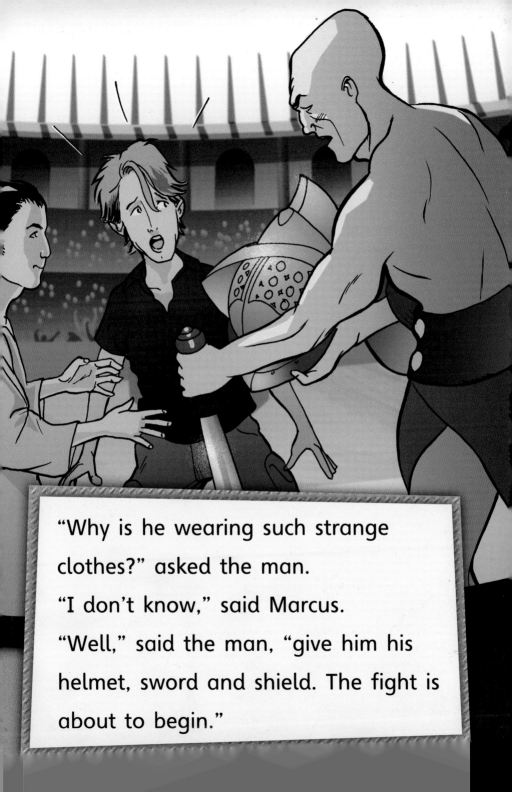

"Why is he wearing such strange clothes?" asked the man.

"I don't know," said Marcus.

"Well," said the man, "give him his helmet, sword and shield. The fight is about to begin."

Marcus gave Scott a helmet, a sword and a shield. The crowd began cheering even louder.

"I've got a bad feeling about this," thought Scott.

Then a big gladiator stormed into the arena. He looked very angry.

"I've got a **very** bad feeling about this," thought Scott.

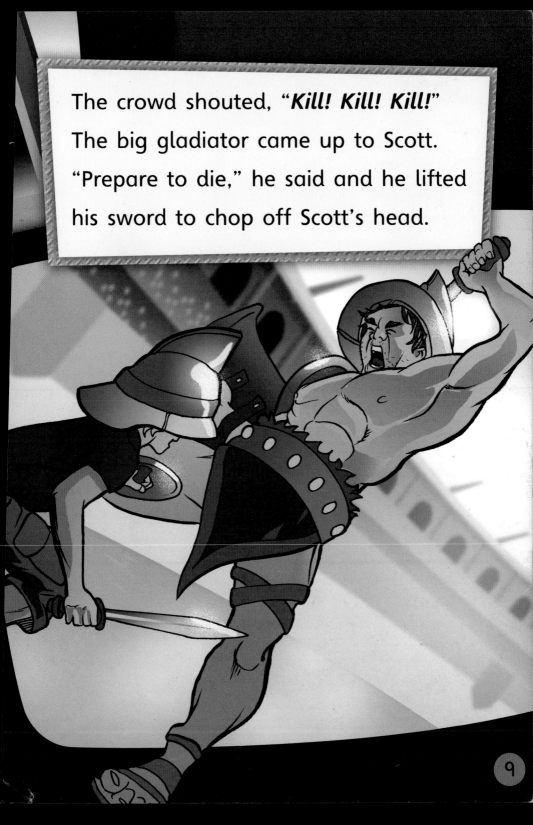

The crowd shouted, "*Kill! Kill! Kill!*"
The big gladiator came up to Scott.
"Prepare to die," he said and he lifted
his sword to chop off Scott's head.

"Oh no you don't, you big bully!" said Scott, and he tried to stab the gladiator. But the sword was so heavy it slipped from Scott's hand. It landed on the gladiator's toe.

"Owwwwww!" yelled the gladiator.
He was hopping around so much that
his helmet slammed shut and he
couldn't see.

Then Scott heard a loud roar and a big lion came into the arena. But to Scott's surprise the lion didn't go for him. It had seen Marcus and Marcus had no helmet, sword or shield!
He looked terrified.

Tigers and leopards were also used in fights.

Scott ran at the lion, waving his sword.
"Get lost, you big bully!" he shouted.
The lion took one look at this mad boy
who was shouting and waving a sword,
then it turned around and ran away.
The crowd cheered and the Emperor
threw a coin to Scott.

"I was right," said Marcus. "You are very brave and strong. You saved my life!"

Scott took off his helmet and shield.

But as Scott gave Marcus his shield,
something very strange happened.
The sun shone on the shield and made
it gleam like a mirror.
Scott looked at the shield and he felt
himself falling forwards.

Scott was back in his bedroom, looking at his old mirror.
The person looking back at Scott was Scott.
"Strange," thought Scott, as he looked at the coin in his hand.

Quiz

- What did Scott have to do in the arena?
- Do you think Scott dreamed he was fighting a gladiator?

Word Detective

- **Phonic Focus:** Identifying long- and short-vowel phonemes

  Page 15: How many syllables are there in the word 'himself'? Is the vowel phoneme in each syllable long or short?
- Page 4: Which two words are contracted in 'we'll'?
- Page 12: Find a word meaning 'very frightened'.

Super Speller

Read these words:

we'll   feeling   shouted

Now try to spell them!

HA! HA! HA!

Q Why did the Romans build straight roads?

A So their soldiers wouldn't go round the bend!

17

Before Reading

Find out about

- Life in ancient Rome

Tricky words

- Colosseum
- gladiators
- feast
- special
- Emperor
- bravely
- sword
- shield

Introduce these tricky words and help the reader when they come across them later!

Text starter

Read about Julius, who lived in Rome in AD 130. It is a feast day and he is going to the Colosseum with his father to see hunters fight with lions, and then two gladiators fighting.

Fight to the Death

My name is Julius. I live in Rome. Today is a very big day for me because my father is taking me to a show at the Colosseum. We are going to see the gladiators fight!

This morning I woke up very early. It is a feast day so I do not have to do any lessons.

A feast day means a holiday.

I had breakfast with my father.
The slave brought us our food.
I ate some bread and some honey.
Then I had some fruit. The slave
cut up my fruit for me.

After breakfast I went to the toilet. There are four seats in our toilet but today I was on my own. That makes a change! I used the sponge stick to clean myself.

There was no such thing as toilet paper in ancient Rome!

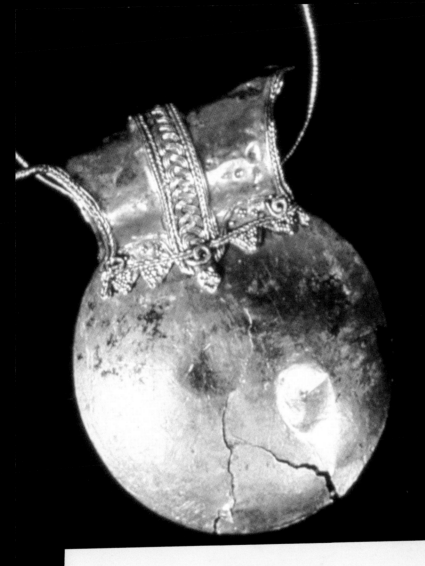

Then I got dressed. I put on my bulla. It is a special locket my father gave me when I was born. Every boy in Rome wears a bulla. It is a good luck charm.

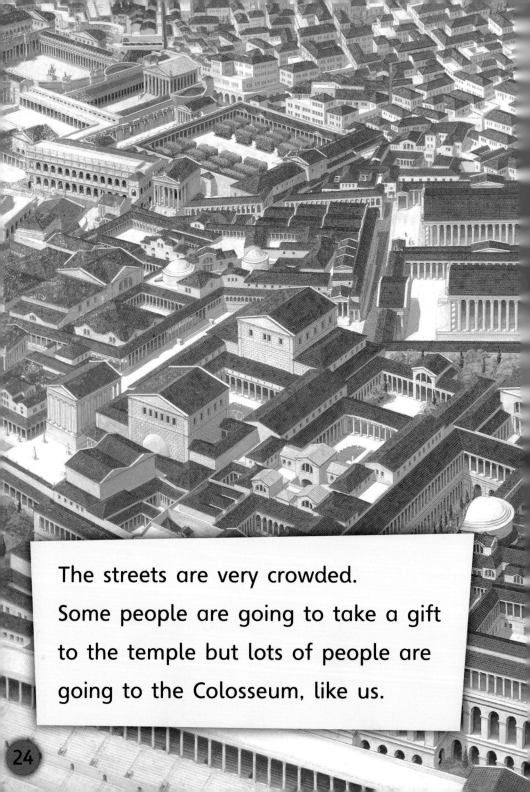

The streets are very crowded.
Some people are going to take a gift
to the temple but lots of people are
going to the Colosseum, like us.

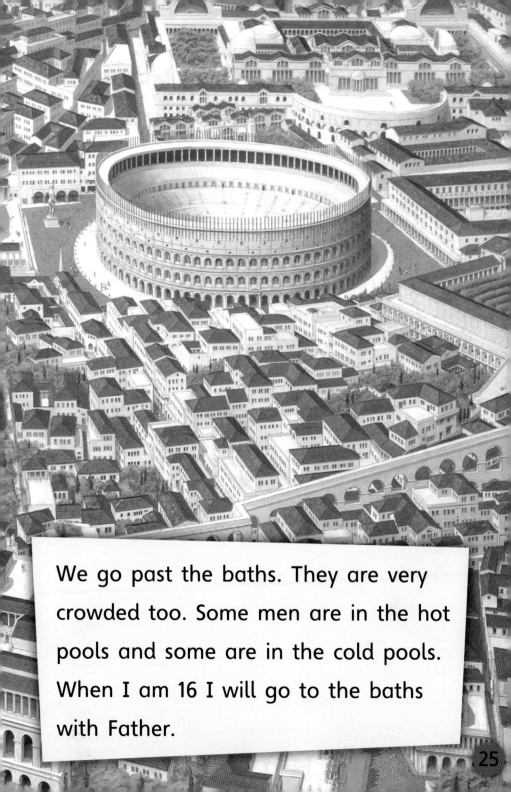

We go past the baths. They are very crowded too. Some men are in the hot pools and some are in the cold pools. When I am 16 I will go to the baths with Father.

At last we get to the Colosseum. It is very crowded. I have never seen so many people. Father says there must be 45,000 people here!

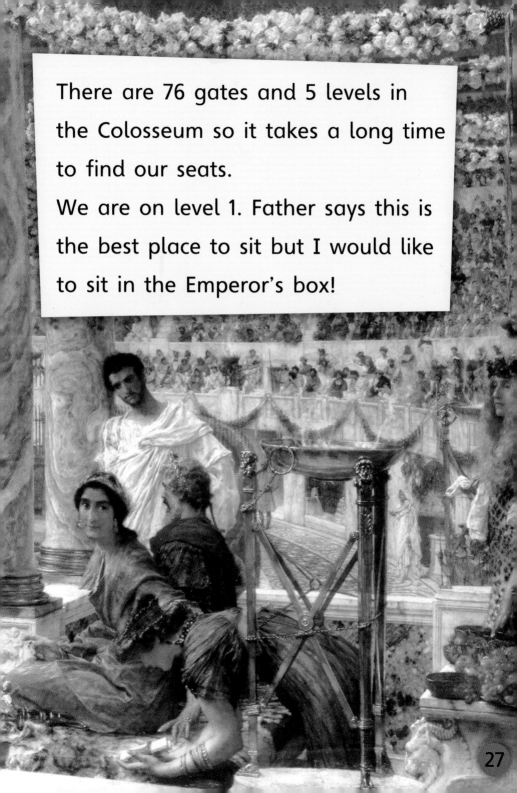

There are 76 gates and 5 levels in the Colosseum so it takes a long time to find our seats.

We are on level 1. Father says this is the best place to sit but I would like to sit in the Emperor's box!

The show begins!

First some elephants enter. I have never seen such strange creatures.

Then a hunter comes in. He is carrying a spear. He is attacked by a lion. He fights bravely but he is killed.

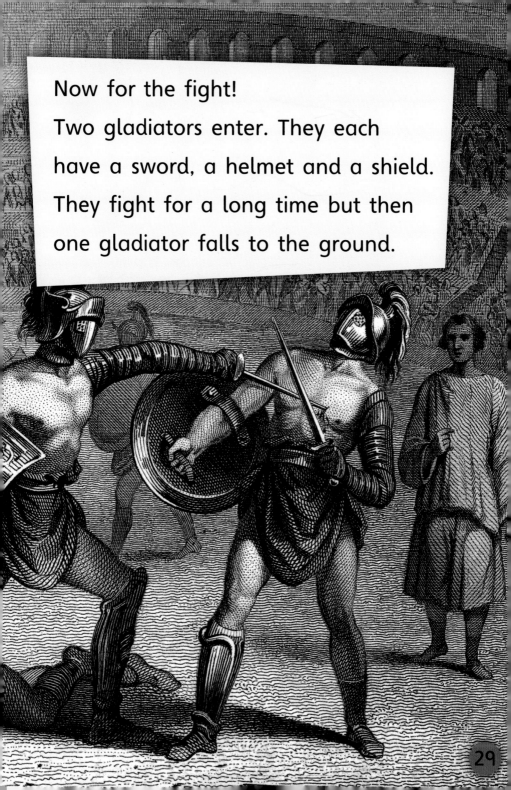

Now for the fight!

Two gladiators enter. They each have a sword, a helmet and a shield. They fight for a long time but then one gladiator falls to the ground.

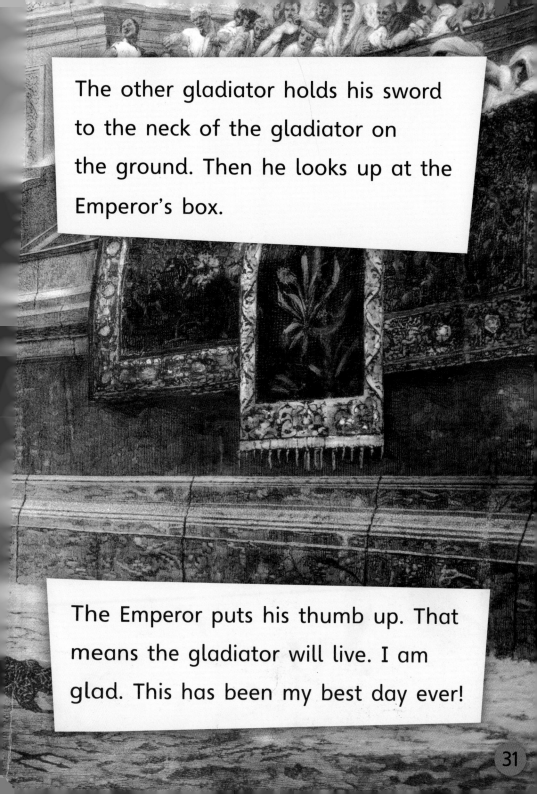

The other gladiator holds his sword to the neck of the gladiator on the ground. Then he looks up at the Emperor's box.

The Emperor puts his thumb up. That means the gladiator will live. I am glad. This has been my best day ever!

Quiz

Text Detective

- What does it mean when the Emperor puts his thumb up?
- Why do you think that Julius said it was his best day ever?

Word Detective

- **Phonic Focus:** Identifying long- and short-vowel phonemes

  Page 22: How many syllables are there in the word 'toilet'? Is the vowel phoneme in each syllable long or short?
- Page 22: How many sentences are there on this page?
- Page 27: Find three plural nouns.

Super Speller

Read these words:

change   carrying   ground

Now try to spell them!

HA! HA! HA!

Q Which month do soldiers hate most?

A March!